ENDLESS
RIVER

ENDLESS RIVER

LI PO AND TU FU:
A FRIENDSHIP IN POETRY

translated by Sam Hamill

WEATHERHILL
New York   Tokyo

Many of these poems originally appeared in *American Poetry Review, Poetry East, Willow Springs,* and *Malahat Review.* Most of these poems were published in *Banished Immortal: Visions of Li T'ai-po* (1987) and *Facing the Snow: Visions of Tu Fu* (1988) by White Pine Press, often in differing form.

First edition, 1993

Published by Weatherhill, Inc., 420 Madison Avenue, 15th Floor, New York, NY 10017. Protected by copyright under terms of the International Copyright Union; all rights reserved. Except for fair use in book reviews, no part of this book may be reproduced for any reason by any means, including any method of photographic reproduction, without permission of the publisher. Printed in the United States.

Library of Congress Cataloging in Publication Data

Endless river/edited by Sam Hamill.—1st ed.
    p.   cm.
  A collection of translated poems of Li Po and Tu Fu.
  ISBN 0-8348-0263-5: $7.95
  1. Chinese poetry—T'ang dynasty, 618–907—Translations into English. 2. Li, Po, 701–762—Translations into English. 3. Tu, Fu, 712–770—Translations into English.
  I. Hamill, Sam. II. Li, Po, 701–762. Poems. English. Selections. 1993. III. Tu, Fu, 712–770. Poems. English. Selections. 1993.
PL2658.E3E54 1993
895.1'108003—dc20   93-13608
                                           CIP

For Eron Hamill,
William O'Daly,
and Gray Foster

CONTENTS

Note that each poem by Li Po begins on the left, and forms a pair with the following poem by Tu Fu, which begins on the right.

ACKNOWLEDGMENTS

Special thanks to Irving Yucheng Lo, J.P. Seaton, and Paul Hansen for their expert comments and clarification while these poems were in manuscript.

INTRODUCTION

The friendship of Li Po (701–762) and Tu Fu (712–770), arguably the two greatest poets of China's greatest literary era, is legendary despite the fact that they spent only one significant period of time together—as much as three months in Sung-chou in 744 with fellow poet Kao Shih—and wrote only a handful of poems to one another over the following twenty years, a period marked by terrible droughts and fires in 750 and 751 and by the An Lu-shan Rebellion, which decimated the capital city of Ch'ang-an and the rest of China in 755 and 756.

It was an odd friendship. Li Po was a braggart, a genius knight-errant, a peerless panhandler, devout Taoist, and a drunk. He married three times: his first wife died young, his second apparently packed up their children and left him, and the third survived him. In his biography of Li Po, Arthur Waley calls him "boastful, callous, dissipated, irresponsible and untruthful." No one contributed more substantially to the legend of Li Po than the poet himself. And yet his poems exhibit one of the most distinctive voices in all of Chinese literature and a mind attuned to Taoist and early Buddhist aesthetics (if not their strict self-discipline).

Tu Fu provides an almost perfect contrast. Born into a genteel literary family in Honan, he owned several farms and was a model of Confucian decorum compared to Li's spontaneous outbursts of "Taoist inspiration." Tu Fu endured enormous hardship, including long exile and a famine in which his own son died. His reverence for life and his compassionate humanity are as legendary as Li Po's behavior, and his poetry is the primary testament to these qualities.

It would be difficult to imagine any two contemporary poets whose work is less alike. Li Po was given to flights of incredible imagination, and he claimed his poems were all written spontaneously under divine inspiration. Tu Fu was and is China's greatest genius of formal invention, a dedicated craftsman who agonized over each line. Unlike his friend, Tu Fu left virtually no erotic poetry. His poems bear witness to an age and are rooted in the poetics of verifiable experience.

While Li Po eventually achieved the fame he so longed for, Tu Fu remained a virtually anonymous poet all his life, the first biography appearing fifty years after his death, and his poems forgotten for nearly three hundred years. If Li Po is the ecstatic Taoist, the showman, Tu Fu is the humble Confucian scholar.

Tu Fu could nevertheless bury a needle in a poem. In "To Li Po on a Spring Day," he praises a poet ten years his elder, "There's no one quite like you, Li Po," or, in (inadequate) literal translation, "Po it is!" This opening line echoes the praise Confucius gave to his disciple Yen Hui. The phrase thus becomes what we might call a left-handed compliment, with Tu Fu claiming the higher Confucian ground for himself.

Li Po's behavior was, at best, unorthodox. He is perhaps the only great poet of the T'ang dynasty who never stood for civil service examinations, probably for lack of a sponsor. Any official sponsoring a candidate would be held accountable for his man's behavior. Legend has it that Li Po died drunk in 762, trying to embrace the reflection of the moon in the Yellow River, but a nearly identical episode appears in the earlier tale of *Monkey*, so was probably part of the poet's myth.

Tu Fu died eight years later, probably of consumption while returning to his home following a period of exile. If Li Po's life is the very stuff of legend, Tu Fu's life is revealed with remarkable clarity in the 1,500 poems—about one-sixth of his life's work—he left behind. Nearly two-thirds of these poems are "regulated verse" (*lu-shih*), eight-line poems composed in five- or seven-syllable lines grouped to form couplets, with the same rhyme used on even-numbered lines. Couplets 2 and 3 form parallelisms, and sometimes double-parallelisms.

Li Po was by contrast a brilliant "organic" poet, a true master not of form, but of inventive imagination and literary theft. He could lift whole lines from extremely well-known poems and make them entirely his own. Everything he wrote, longer narrative poems and brief lyrics, sounds exactly like Li Po and no one else.

Translating two poets so remarkably different, I have struggled—sometimes perhaps vainly—to retain some of the distinctive qualities of each voice. But adding prepositions, pronouns, articles and conjunctions, and engaging the musical ear of American English, the translator becomes, among other things, a filter through which the *poetry* flows. The result is a conversation, wholly imagined by the translator, in which two poets speak only in answering poems.

Many of these poems are "occasional" in the best sense, and because of the context in which they are presented, I have left out footnotes and other scholarly apparatus in favor of presenting the poems *as poems* only. There is plenty of wonderful scholarship available for the study of T'ang poets: anything by Burton Watson, Kenneth Rexroth, Arthur Waley, Stephen Owen, J. P. Seaton, or David Hinton comes very highly recommended. Naturally, scholarship improves the quality of one's reading, but for this particular context, a sense of intimacy is essential.

I like to think of the two of them coming to my little cedar house in the woods near where the Strait of Juan de Fuca opens into Puget Sound. Both are elderly, but in good health and high spirits. We have few "modern" conveniences—they would disrupt the true experience of the poetry—but we have candles and lamps and plentiful wine.

It is autumn, as it is autumn in the lives of the three men gathered here. Whatever is actually said between the poets will be left to any eavesdropper to imagine. I bank the fire after dinner, heat rice wine, and listen to light rain falling through hundred-foot evergreens.

We are three old men with a little time to remember, to reminisce in verse, to call back a few moments from along the many, many miles we have each traveled—most often alone. The poems are spoken slowly, and sometimes recited more than once. And there is an appropriate length of silence between, unlike the modern public poetry reading. The silence is as important as the poems themselves, is a part of the poetry, and we relish it.

Li Po, being the eldest, begins—of course!—with a salutation.

POEMS BY
LI PO
AND
TU FU

ABOUT TU FU

I met Tu Fu on a mountaintop
in August when the sun was hot.

Under the shade of his big straw hat,
his face was sad—

In the years since we'd last parted,
he'd grown wan, exhausted.

Poor old Tu Fu, I thought then,
he must be agonizing over poetry again.

—Li Po

TO LI PO on a Spring Day

There's no poet quite like you, Li Po,
you live in my imagination.

You sing as sweet as Yin,
and still retain Pao's nobility.

Under spring skies north of the Wei,
you wander into the sunset

toward the village of Chiang-tung.
Tell me, will we ever again

buy another keg of wine
and argue over prosody and rhyme?

—Tu Fu

SAYING GOODBYE in a Ch'in-ling Wineshop

Spring winds perfume the shop
with heavy blooming catkins.

A girl from Wu pours wine
and encourages our drinking.

With friends from the city
I come to toast and say goodbye.

About to part, I point them toward
the great east-churling river.

Can any river possibly flow
beyond the love of friends?

—Li Po

TO LI PO on a Winter Day

Alone in my secluded hut,
I think of you all day, Li Po.

Whenever I read of friendship,
I remember your friendly poems.

Harsh winds tatter your old clothes
as you search for the wine of endless life.

Unable to go with you, I remember only
that old hermitage we'd hoped to make a home.

—Tu Fu

LISTENING to a Flute on a Spring Night in
Lo-yang

A few dark notes from a jade flute
disappear into the spring breezes of Lo-yang.

At midnight, hearing "Willow-breaking Song,"
is there a soul who does not think of home?

—Li Po

ANOTHER SPRING

In all the country, only the landscape is firm.
It is springtime in the city. Weeds cover everything,

trees overgrown, flowers watered with our tears
until even the birds have learned to moan.

Beacon fires of war have lit the hills for months.
I'd give anything for a letter.

I scratch my poor white head and hair falls out,
and my hair's already so thin it can barely hold a
hairpin.

—Tu Fu

*Sheng Mou (fl. c. 1310–61): Boating on the River in Autumn.
Section of a handscroll, ink and colors on paper (H. 9 3/4").
Palace Museum Collection, Taichung.*

SEEING Off a Friend

Yesterday has flown, leaving only its sorrows.
That and the sorrows of today fill my heart with longing.
Autumn geese vanish in the wind.

I watch from the tower with my cup, thinking:
the old formal poets, the new who write in a casual way—
how they all love high-minded ideals.

Wanting to touch Heaven, they embrace the moon.
Drawing my sword to cut water, the water flows;
filling my cup to drown sorrow, the sorrows all return.

This life, this world, is struggle.
You'll let down your hair
and take to your boat tomorrow.

—Li Po

THINKING of Li Po

A cold wind out of the wilderness.
What would you recommend?

When will the wild goose bring news
from the Lakes-and-Rivers land?

Poets must live without success,
driven by demons.

Remember the ghost of poor Ch'u Yuan—
send him a poem down the river.

—Tu Fu

SAYING GOODBYE to Meng Hao-jan at Yellow Crane Pavilion

You said goodbye at Yellow Crane Pavilion
and sailed west, down into the valley
through the flowers and mists of spring
until your lonely sail vanished
in the blue sky's horizon,

and I was left watching the river
flowing gently into heaven.

—Li Po

IN A VILLAGE by the River

The clear river curves around our village:
these long summer days are beautiful, indeed.

Swallows swoop from the eaves,
the gulls all flock to the water.

My wife draws a rice-paper Go board
while our sons bend fish-hooks from needles.

This medicine is all a sick man needs.
What man could ask for more?

—Tu Fu

IN A VILLAGE by the River

The rain stops falling in this river village.
And now, the wine gone, you say goodbye.

Comfortable in your little boat,
you ride sails homeward on the water,

passing islands burning up with flowers,
passing slender river willows.

And what of the one you leave behind?
I return to my rock and my fishing line.

—Li Po

EVENING After Rain

Sudden winds brought rain this afternoon
to save my thirsty garden.

Now sunset steams the grass
and the river softly glistens.

Who'll organize my scattered books?
Tonight I'll fill and fill my glass.

I know they love to talk about me.
But no one faults me for my reclusive life.

—Tu Fu

I MAKE MY HOME in the Mountains

You ask why I live
alone in the mountain forest,

and I smile and am silent
until even my soul grows quiet:

it lives in the other world,
one that lies beyond men.

The peach trees blossom.
The water continues to flow.

—Li Po

NIGHT THOUGHTS While Traveling

Thin grass bends on the breezy shore,
and the tall mast seems lonely in my boat.

Stars ride low across the wide plain,
and the moon is tossed by the Yangtze.

What is fame and literary status—
the old and infirm should leave office.

Adrift, drifting, what is left for the lone gull
adrift between earth and heaven.

—Tu Fu

DRINKING ALONE with the Moon

I take my wine jug out among flowers
to drink alone, without friends.
I raise my cup to entice the moon.
That, and my shadow, make us three.

But the moon doesn't drink,
and my shadow follows silently.
Still, shadow and moon for companions,
I travel to the ends of spring.

When I sing, the moon dances.
When I dance, my shadow dances too.
Sober, we share life's joys;
drunk, each goes a separate way.

Constant companions although we wander,
we'll meet again in the Milky Way.

—Li Po

SUNSET

How beautiful the river is in spring
with sunset filling the window.

The garden on the bank is sweet,
and so is the smoke of the boatmen.

Sparrows squabble in the branches,
insects buzz through my court.

Ah, heady unstrained wine—one cup,
and a thousand griefs will vanish.

—Tu Fu

MOUNTAIN Drinking Song

To drown the ancient sorrows,
we drank a hundred jugs of wine

there in beautiful moonlight. We couldn't
go to bed with the moon so bright.

Then finally the wine overcame us
and we lay down on the empty mountain:

earth for a pillow
and a blanket made of heaven.

—Li Po

MOONLIT NIGHT

This same moon hangs over Fu-chou.
Alone, she'll lean out her window to watch it.

Our poor children are too small
to even remember Chang-an.

Dew will dampen her perfumed hair.
Clear moonlight makes her bare arms cool.

Will we ever sit again in her window,
the tears finally gone from our faces?

—Tu Fu

WOMEN of Yueh (1)

The woman from Ch'ang-an
has eyes more beautiful than the moon,
bare feet white as frost
without the stockings of the upper-crust.

—Li Po

I STAND ALONE

A falcon hovers at the edge of the sky.
Two gulls drift slowly up the river.

Vulnerable while they ride the wind,
they coast and glide with ease.

Dew is heavy on the grass below,
the spider's web is ready.

Heaven's ways include the affairs of man:
among a thousand sorrows, I stand alone.

—Tu Fu

Wu Chen (1280–1354): Fishermen. Section of a handscroll, ink on paper (H. 12 3/16 "). Freer Gallery of Art, Washington, D.C.

WOMEN of Yueh (2)

Southern women have alabaster skin,
and this one steers her boat for play.
Springtime dances in her eyes
when she picks water lilies
to give to romantic passersby.

—Li Po

CROOKED RIVER Meditation

Each falling petal diminishes spring.
Ten thousand of them sadden me.

Spring flowers pale, and I grieve,
and ease my remorse with wine.

Kingfishers nest in the temple hall,
there is a stone unicorn on a royal grave.

Taking my pleasures where I find them,
I fill my cup again.

—Tu Fu

WOMEN of Yueh (3)

Gathering lotuses by Yeh River,
she sings whenever someone passes,
then quickly hides her boat among the lilies—
so coy, pretending shyness.

—Li Po

MOON ON THE COLD Food Festival

Homeless on Cold Food Festival Day,
I have nothing but this river of my tears.

If I cut down the moon's one cassia tree,
wouldn't the moonlight be brighter?

When red flowers bloom for lonely lovers,
her brow will be knit by sorrows.

No complaints. Like Cowboy and Weaving Girl,
we'll cross the river in autumn.

—Tu Fu

BLUE WATER

He drifts on blue water under a clear moon,
picking white lilies on South Lake.

Every lotus blossom speaks of love
until his heart will break.

—Li Po

RANDOM PLEASURES (4)

Blown by winds, the thistledown
drifts where it will, falling

through a thousand feet of frozen sky
to find another world.

The crooked path to my old home
has been deserted three long years.

Far off, the beacon flares blaze up—
chariots and weapons flood the eastern pass.

How long is one man's time on earth?
How long must the life of a wanderer last?

—Tu Fu

*Hsia Kuei (fl. c. 1190–1230): A Pure and Remote View of
Rivers and Mountains. Section of a handscroll, ink on paper
(H. 18 1/4"). Palace Museum Collection, Taichung.*

PARTING

We cross the river narrows
and continue deep into the land of Chu.

Soon the mountains drop onto a plain
the river crosses, flowing into Heaven.

The moon reflects the wide, blank sky;
clouds rise into terraces and towers.

Goodbye. You ride the waters of our home
though you sail ten thousand miles.

—Li Po

BY YANGTZE and Han

Wandering beside rivers, I remember my home
between heaven and earth, an aging exiled scholar.

Only a smeared ghost of a cloud
and a pale moon in the long night sky.

The sun has set in my heart.
Autumn winds rise up around my sickbed.

Even the old horse has its stall in the barn
though he's too old for the road.

—Tu Fu

TAKING LEAVE of a Friend

Green mountains rise to the north;
white water rolls past the eastern city.

Once it has been uprooted,
the tumbleweed travels forever.

Drifting clouds like a wanderer's mind;
sunset, like the heart of your old friend.

We turn, pause, look back and wave.
Even our ponies look back and whine.

—Li Po

RIVER PAVILION

I lie out flat on the river pavilion,
reciting poems or dreaming.

Water roars by, but my heart grows still.
Clouds drift over and my mind responds as lazily.

Nothing moves in springtime dusk.
Such joy in the secret want of things.

How can I retire to my forest home again?
To dispel my melancholy, I write another poem.

—Tu Fu

SPRINGTIME South of the Yangtze

The time of green spring winds returns.
The orioles will not stop singing.

My hair grows white on the banks of the Yangtze,
my home far beyond the mountains.

My heart soars with the clouds of Chin
while the moon casts my shadow in Chu.

Having squandered my life,
my garden is buried in weeds.

This late—so many years gone by—
nothing left but to sing alone

beyond the imperial gate.

—Li Po

SONG OF THE WAR WAGONS

Wagons clang and horses cry
as soldiers pass with bows and arrows.
Families clamor to watch them go.
A huge cloud of dust swallows the trembling bridge.
Clinging to their clothes, they weep and stumble by,
their cries echoing through the sky.

And if you questioned them, they would say,
"Conscripted at fifteen, we fought for the north;
now almost forty, we move to fight in the west.
Once, villagers gave us honors;
now we return white-haired, heading toward frontiers.
We've shed a sea of blood.
Still the emperor wants more.
East of the mountains, a thousand villages,
ten thousand villages, turn to bitter weeds.

Wang Meng (c. 1309–1385): Forest Dwellings at Chü-Ch'ü. Hanging scroll, ink and colors on paper (27 x 16¾"). Palace Museum Collection, Taichung.

Even when strong women work the fields,
our canals and crops are feeble.
The warriors of Ch'in fight on,
driven like dogs and cattle.

You may ask, but we don't dare complain.
This winter we await new troops
while officials raise new taxes.
But where will the money come from?
We've learned the grief of raising sons—
not like the quiet joy of daughters
we can marry to our neighbors.
Our boys lie under the weeds.
Near Kokonor, their old white bones
remain with no one to collect them.
Old ghosts and new complaints: you can hear them
all night long through falling mist and rain.

—Tu Fu

OLD-STYLE POEM

I climbed Lotus Mountain in the west
to see in the distance a bright star girl
whose pale hand held a lotus.
She stepped from emptiness to emptiness,
her skirts a belted rainbow
sashaying in the breeze that bore her up
into the heavens, and from there she called
to me to climb to her cloud terrace,
saluting the immortals. Stunned,
I stood stark still and watched
her ride a swan into purple darkness.

I looked down only then on the Lo-yang River:
teeming with Tartar troops,
meadows rivered with blood,
wolves and jackals wearing the caps of men.

Li Po

THE THATCHED HUT

When barbarians overran the city,
I abandoned my old thatched hut.

But now the city is peaceful once again,
and at last I can come back.

The rebellion broke in a flash—
planned to be ruthless and sudden.

With our general off to visit the Court,
his hirelings conspired;

they sacrificed a beautiful white stallion
and swore their oath in its blood.

Some rode west to conscript our army;
some closed the road to the north;

some, particularly vile,
even named themselves to office.

But when the barbarians challenged them for power,
these traitors were afraid.

In the west, the army mutinied,
rebel killing rebel—

who could have guessed their deaths
would come from their own cruel legion—

and all decent people grieved
at a world plunged into chaos.

Petty officials multiplied,
and thousands became their victims.

Their terrorist hirelings, indiscriminate,
murdered innocent and innocent alike,

amused themselves with torture
performed to chamber music,

and ordered death with a laugh.
The streets were sewers of blood.

You still can hear their cries—
there where the axes fell.

The rebels plundered freely,
stealing horses, enslaving women—

and where was the Empire then?
We were afraid and broken-hearted.

I had no choice—I ran.
And longed three years for the coast.

Arrows filled the air above the Yangtze.
And I longed for the Five Lakes region.

A life away is not a life—
I return to attack my weeds.

Inside the gate, my four strong pines.
I stroll through my bamboo grove.

My old dog yips and leaps,
darting in and out of my robe.

*T'ang Yin (1470–1523): Secluded Fishermen on an Autumn River.
Section of a handscroll, ink and colors on silk (H. 11 ½"). Palace
Museum Collection, Taichung.*

My neighbors rush out to greet me
with bottles of sweet rice wine.

Even the governor sends greetings
by an official, to assess my needs.

Our whole village celebrates,
my neighbors and my friends,

but still there's no place in the world.
We honor more soldiers than poets.

Between the wind and the dust,
is there room for a poor man's life?

I live like a parasite—
happily, happy just to be alive.

If I've not earned my food and wine,
let all the worst be mine.

—Tu Fu

RISING DRUNK on a Spring Day

This world's a dream, so why
a lifetime of suffering?
I end the day ruinously drunk,
asleep on the porch till I wake confused.

An oriole explores the flowers
and I ask, "Say, friend,
what season is it now?"
and it sings of spring breezes.

Moved almost to tears,
I lie down again with my wine
to compose a bright moon song,
but the feeling's gone before the song is done.

—Li Po

FACING THE SNOW

New ghosts weep over lost battles.
Alone and cold, I recite a litany of woes.

Heavy clouds rumble into the sunset,
quick snow dancing in the winds.

Imperfect, the smith's new ladle lies discarded,
but his fire still throbs red.

No news. Are all the provinces still there?
I write out my sorrows in air.

—Tu Fu

FALL RIVER SONG

Along Fall River, gibbons cry all night,
and Yellow Mountain has long white hair.

Blue Creek will never flood
like the rivers of my home.

My heart sinks in the river,
drowns in the longing to go home.

Am I doomed to wander forever?
These tears will swamp my boat.

—Li Po

DREAMING of Li Po

1

Parted by death, we could stifle our tears;
parting in life, we've memories to cling to.

There is pestilence south of the river,
you are exiled, and I have not a word.

Old friend, I see you only in dreams,
but you know my heart is with you.

It's not the same as having your living spirit:
that road's too long to be measured.

Your spirit is in the heart of the green maple,
your spirit returns to the dark frontier.

Tangled in the nets of law, tell me,
how can the spirit soar?

Moonlight fills my room. Your poor face
shines, reflected in the rafters.

The waters are deep, the waves wide.
May peaceful serpents pass you by.

2

All day, huge clouds roll by.
You, exile, must travel.

Three nights I dreamed of you,
I dreamed we were together.

"I try, I try," you say, "but
this bitter road is difficult to travel:

winds drive lakes and rivers into waves,
my boat and oars would fail."

Leaving, you smoothed your long white hair
like a man who embraced his failures.

In Ch'ang-an, they lavish praise on officials
while you endure and endure.

They say that Heaven's net is wide.
We're tangled in the web of aging.

Your fame will last ten thousand years
though you are silent, vanished from this world.

—Tu Fu

IN MEMORY of Ho Chi-chen

People in his homeland thought him mad,
so Ho Chi-chen wandered with the winds.

When we first met in Ch'ang-an,
he dubbed me the "Banished Immortal."

He loved good talk and his cup,
who lies under bamboo and pine.

Through a veil of tears, I see
poor Ho, hocking his ring for wine.

—Li Po

SONG of T'ung-ku

Already old, and still without a name,
I've starved three years in these mountains.

The ministers of Ch'ang-an all are young,
their money and honors earned.

My friends, the mountain sages,
dwell only on the past, in their hurting.

I chant this last song sadly, my eyes
on the August sky where the white sun races.

—Tu Fu

FAREWELL to Yin Shu

The moon rises over White Heron Island.
At dawn, we will say a last farewell.

Already skies grow lighter, sun behind
Green Dragon Hill pushing up through clouds.

This flowing river feels nothing.
Winds will fill sails that carry him away.

Silenced by sadness, we can only watch,
then lift our cups, honoring old vows.

—Li Po

DRINKING at Crooked River

Beyond the park, at River's Head,
the water's calm, the palace disappears.

Peach and willow blossoms scatter
as orioles fly up together.

Drinking, I don't care what they say—
I never cared for the courts.

From my office I now see the immortals
have long since sunk into the sea.

Old and grieved, I see it's futile
to lament the duties I evaded.

—Tu Fu

DRINKING WINE with a Mountain Hermit

We sit together among
blossoming mountain flowers,

drinking cup after cup
until I'm so drunk

I grow drowsy.
You, old friend, must leave

come tomorrow, if you choose,
but don't forget your lute.

—Li Po

POEM FOR MR. LI in Early Spring

Though sick, I rise at dawn—
your poem, Grief in Early Spring, has come.

It multiplies the autumns in my heart
and I realize old age has found me.

Tender peach-buds all blush red,
the willow shoots turn green.

Night after night, I dream of time, but
within Four Seas, only the dust and the wind.

—Tu Fu

TO A FRIEND

Late autumn strips the distant hills
beyond the city gate.

A huge white cloud interrupts my dreams
and returns me to this world.

And you, old friend?
Flown silent as a crane.

Will you ever return
to your old home again?

—Li Po

SPRING HOMECOMING

Through tall bamboo the mossy path
winds down to the easy river.

Flowers bloom beneath the eaves
of the ancient wide-thatched hall.

After months away,
I come back home in spring,

leaning on my cane
to look at flowers and stones,

packing my wine jar down
to walk and drink on the beach.

Gulls swim and dive in the distance,
swallows wrestle with the wind.

The world's ways are difficult, indeed,
but every life has its limits.

Sobering up, I drink again:
stoned, I finally feel at home.

—Tu Fu

REMEMBERING East Mountain

It's been forever since I returned to walk
the trails of my East Mountain home.

How many roses bloomed alone,
white clouds gathered only to be blown?

Who lives there now and stays up late
to watch this bright moon go down?

—Li Po

HEAVENLY RIVER

Heavenly River is year-round muddy
except in the clarity of autumn,

when a few small clouds make shadows,
but it's always bright at night.

The stars that swim the river shine on the capital
dome.
The river carries off the moon to set beyond the
border.

Cowboy and Weaving Girl cross the river each
autumn
and neither wind nor wave can stop them.

—Tu Fu

FALL RIVER SONG (2)

On Old River Mountain
a huge boulder swept clean
by the blue winds of heaven

where they have written
in an alphabet of moss
an ancient song.

—Li Po

DRAGON GATE GORGE

Dragon Gate cuts a wide gorge.
Trees line the road from the city gate,

and the Imperial Palace is imposing.
The temples are silver and gold.

The seasons shift. I come and go,
the lands and waters roll on.

Of all those I met along this road,
will I ever meet any again?

—Tu Fu

GOING TO VISIT a Taoist Recluse on Heaven's
Mountain Only to Find Him Gone

Dogs bark where the river sings
and peach blossoms grow heavy with rain.

Deer wander through woods so deep
I cannot hear the noon-bell near the river.

Bamboo grows thick in blue-green mists
when the rivers plunges from the summit.

No one here to tell me where you've gone,
I linger, pining in the forest.

—Li Po

TO ABBOT MIN the Compassionate

Has it really been thirty years?
Writing this, I can't choke back the tears.

Are you still the servant of culture?
And who can an old man sing to?

Who packs your heavy Go board up the hill?
I remember your robe as our boat drifted on the
    water.

Now, they say, I've a future in office.
Me, a white old head dozing, drinking, dozing off
    again.

—Tu Fu

QUIET NIGHT Thoughts

A pool of moonlight on my bed this late hour
like a blanket of frost on the world.

I lift my eyes to a bright mountain moon.
Resigned, remembering my home, I bow.

—Li Po

MOON, RAIN, Riverbank

Rain roared through, now the autumn night is clear.
The water wears a patina of gold
and carries a bright jade star.
Heavenly River runs clear and pure,
as gently as before.

Sunset buries the mountains in shadow.
A mirror floats in the deep green void,
its light reflecting the cold, wet dusk,
dew glistening,
freezing on the flowers.

—Tu Fu

LISTENING TO A FLUTE in Yellow Crane Pavilion

I came here as a wanderer
thinking of home,
remembering my faraway Ch'ang-an.

And then, from deep in Yellow Crane Pavilion,
I heard a beautiful bamboo flute
play "Falling Plum Blossoms."

It was late summer in a city by a river.

—Li Po

CH'IANG VILLAGE

Western clouds, hill above hill,
vermilion poured over the sunset,
and the sun walks into the earth.
Birds sing everywhere at my hermitage
as I return, suddenly old and weary.

It's a wonder I survive.
My wife and children weep.
The winds have blown me away
and waves have washed me back.
I'm lucky to be alive.

Neighbors swarm over our wall
sighing, crying, carrying on.
Red-eyed with our tears,
we light the evening candle—
together we enter the dream.

—Tu Fu

WATERFALL at Lu-shan

Sunlight steams the river stones.
From high above, the river steadily plunges—

three thousand feet of sparkling water—
the Milky Way pouring down from Heaven.

—Li Po

EVENING NEAR Serpent River

Breezes sigh, rising over bright tiled steps,
the round sun sinks below the wall.

Wild autumn geese slowly vanish
as sunset lengthens all the clouds.

Leaves have begun to drop already.
Cold flowers lose their fragrance.

I add my tears to the river.
At slacktide, only the moon is pure.

—Tu Fu

*Attributed to Mu-ch'i (fl. mid-thirteenth century): Evening Glow
on a Fishing Village, from Eight Views of the Hsiao-Hsiang
Region. Section of a handscroll, ink on paper (H. 13"). Nezu Art
Museum, Tokyo.*

LOOKING FOR MASTER Yung Ts'un Near His Hermitage

You live where green mountains reach almost
to the sky, indifferent to the passing years.

Here where the old road disappears into
drifting clouds, I linger awhile by the river.

Dark oxen lie among the wildflowers;
high in pines, white cranes silently doze.

As I walk, twilight falls on the river and I
return alone, down through mist and cold.

—Li Po

FACING THE SNOW (2)

Northern snows invade the city,
northern clouds have frozen all the homes.

Hard winds mix leaves with snow,
cold rains erase the flowers.

Once again, no money. I wonder
if I could get wine on credit.

But without a friend to share it,
I'll wait for sunset and the crows.

—Tu Fu

CROWS at Dusk

In the yellow-cloud dusk, the crows
return to their nests near the city wall,
and as they settle, they call.

Alone at her loom in Ch'ang-an,
a girl weaves beautiful brocade.
But for whom?

Behind her gauze curtain,
she mutters as she works,
and when her shuttle finally stops,

she sulks, recalling her lover again.
She lies alone in bed all night.
And her poor tears rain.

—Li Po

IN SECLUSION

It is evening before I rise.
Out of work, I find the house is peaceful.

Bamboo surrounds the wilds
and the water reflects my cottage.

My sons are lazy boors,
my wife complains of constant poverty.

I'd like to be drunk a hundred years.
It's already been a month since I even combed my
    hair.

—Tu Fu

SUMMER DAYS in the Mountains

Too lazy even to move a feather fan,
stripped naked in the deep green forest,

even my headband left on a stone wall somewhere,
I let the pine winds ruffle my hair.

—Li Po

GOING TO THE PALACE with a Friend at Dawn

The water-clock marks dawn,
the peach blossoms rosy as wine.

Dragons and snakes on banners snap in the warm
    morning sun.
Sparrows and swallows glide on palace breezes.

I can smell the palace incense on your sleeve.
Poems should drip from your brush like pearls.

Who influences the court more than one generation?
Another pheasant feather floats in the palace pool.

—Tu Fu

AT CH'ANG-MEN Palace

This palace was once magnificent,
but now there's only one old woman

who doesn't know spring from autumn.
In a palace built of gold.

Heavy with dust, no one cleans it.
And the only visitor at night

is this huge lonely moon,
tracing the walls with its fingers.

—Li Po

TO A GUEST

Spring waters run north and south from here,
but we have only the gulls for guests.

Now you've climbed our bramble path
and entered our rough wood gate.

This far from town, our cooking isn't fancy.
Stale rice wine is all a poor man has to offer.

Sit here. I'll fetch my ancient neighbor
to come and help us drink it.

—Tu Fu

ON DRAGON HILL

Drunk on Dragon Hill tonight,
that banished immortal, Great White,

turns among yellow flowers,
his smile spread wide

as his hat sails off on the wind
and he dances away in the moonlight.

—Li Po

AFTER RAIN

At Heaven's Border, the autumn clouds are thin
and driven from the west by a thousand winds.

The world is beautiful at dawn after rain,
and the rains won't hurt the farmers.

Border willows grow kingfisher green,
the hills grow red with mountain pears.

A Tartar lament rises from the tower.
A single wild goose sails into the void.

—Tu Fu

RETURN of the Banished

You return on currents and tides
after years in the wilds of the East.

How many are the sorrows of exile?
More than pearls in the seas.

—Li Po

AFTER THE HARVEST

The rice is cut and clouds glisten in the fields.
Facing Stone Gate, the river is low.

Winds shriek, ripping leaves from shrubs and trees.
At dawn, the pigs and chickens scatter.

Out of the distance, I hear the first sounds of battle.
The woodcutter's song is over. Soon he will leave the
    village.

Homeless and old, I long for word from the homeland.
A wanderer, I place my trust in the world.

—Tu Fu

TO THE TUNE: Beautiful Barbarian

Smoky mist weaves through cold mountain forests
leaving only a belt of heart-rending green.

Twilight covers the tower
where I grieve alone in Jade Pavilion.

All the birds hurry home.
But how shall I find a way?

Long respite, brief respite,
traveling hard, day by day.

—Li Po

PASSING MR. SUNG'S Old House

Mr. Sung's old house collapses.
The pond is full of moss.

I wandered here as a boy,
and was invited to leave a poem.

Old neighbors tell me stories now
until we lapse, at last, into silence.

The old oak looms like an aging general.
Sunset. Winds grieve its trembling leaves.

—Tu Fu

WOMEN of Yueh (5)

Mirror Lake's waters are moon-clear,
and the woman from Yeh River
has a face pale as snow
that trembles in the ripples.

—Li Po

HOMESTEAD

My homestead lies beside a clear stream,
its wicker gate on an unused road.

Deep grass hides it from the marketplace.
It's so secluded, I don't even have to dress.

Branch upon branch, the willows droop;
Tree after tree, the loquats still smell sweet.

Sunset reflects the fishing cormorants,
drying their beautiful black wings.

—Tu Fu

*Tai Chin (fl. early fifteenth century): Fishermen on the River.
Detail from a handscroll, ink and colors on paper (H. 18 ⅛").
Freer Gallery of Art, Washington, D.C.*

ANCIENT AIRS

Climbing high to look out upon the world—
all heaven and earth so very wide,
an autumn cloak of frost on everything,
these strong cold winds promise winter.

There is glory in the east-flowing river,
our concerns are only tiny waves.
Even the white sun is swallowed by clouds,
and the clouds drift on without rest.

Common sparrows roost high in wu-t'ung trees
while phoenixes nest in brambles.
Nothing left but to ramble home again,
tapping my sword to the tune, "Hard Traveling."

—Li Po

TO MY YOUNG BROTHER (of whom I've learned
nothing in four years)

I've heard from strangers you may be living
in a Hangchou mountain temple.

The dusty winds of war prolong our separation,
and now I've spent another autumn beside the
    Yangtze and the Han.

My shadow passes under trees filled with screaming
    monkeys,
but my heart turns down toward the dragons at the
    river-mouth.

When spring waters rise, may they carry me down
to search for you in the east where the white clouds
    end.

—Tu Fu

RESENTMENT near the Jade Steps

Dew whitens the jade steps.
This late, it soaks her gauze stockings.

She lowers her crystal blind to watch
the breaking, glass-clear moon of autumn.

—Li Po

LONE WILD GOOSE

Alone, the wild goose refuses food and drink,
his calls searching for the flock.

Who feels compassion for that single shadow,
vanishing in a thousand distant clouds?

You watch, even as it flies from sight,
its plaintive calls cutting through you.

The noisy crows ignore it:
the bickering, squabbling multitudes.

—Tu Fu

OLD DUST

We live our lives as wanderers
until, dead, we finally come home.

One quick trip between heaven and earth,
then the dust of ten thousand generations.

The Moon-Rabbit mixes elixirs for nothing.
The Tree of Long Life is kindling.

Dead, our white bones lie silent
when pine trees lean toward spring.

Remembering, I sigh; looking ahead, I sigh once
    more:
This life is mist. What fame? What glory?

—Li Po

TRAVELER'S PAVILION

Sunrise brightens my autumn window.
Winds have once again stripped trees.

The morning sun slips between cold mountains,
and the river runs through last night's mist.

Our court makes use of everything it can,
but what's the use of a sick old man?

And what of my one life remains,
rising or falling on autumn winds.

—Tu Fu

ZAZEN ON Ching-t'ing Mountain

The birds have vanished down the sky.
Now the last cloud drains away.

We sit together, the mountain and I,
until only the mountain remains.

—Li Po

LISTLESS

I can't bear a journey to the village—
I'm too contented here.
I call my son to close the wooden gate.

Thick wine drunk in quiet woods, green moss,
jade gray water under April winds—
and beyond: the simmering dusk of the wild.

—Tu Fu

*Ch'iu Ying (c. 1510–51): Landscape in the Manner of Li T'ang.
Section of a handscroll, ink and colors on paper (H. 10"). Freer
Gallery of Art, Washington, D.C.*

LONGING FOR SOMEONE

Longing for someone
in Ch'ang-an—
the crickets sing on the autumn
near the golden well.

Frosty winds bring a chill,
and my futon's the color of cold.
The lamp has burned low
and I am exhausted by longing.

I open the curtain to watch the moon,
but my sighs are all in vain.

She who is lovely as all the flowers
remains beyond the distant clouds.
The heavens are deep blue and endless;
below, the waves are pale.

The sky has no end, like my journey.
We suffer as we go.
Even dreams cannot cross over
the vast mountains that divide us.

And this eternal longing
can turn a heart to dust.

—Li Po

Ch'en Hung-shou (1599–1652): Boating on the Lake. Album leaf, ink and colors on paper (13 ¹/₈ x 10 ³/₄"). J.P. Dubosc Collection, Lugano.

AFTER SOLSTICE

After solstice, sunlight slowly lengthens.
From Two-Edged Sword Trail,
my thoughts return to Lo-yang once again.
Neither my official robe
nor big white horse mean a thing—
Not even a valley of gold and bronze camels
when I am so far from home.

Plum blossoms? I don't see a thing.
Mountain cherry and sweet blossom severed,
each aches, longing for the other
like two separated brothers.
Sorrows weigh me down when poems
should touch the roots of joy to rouse it.
But with each poem completed, chanting,
that old, cold ache resumes.

—Tu Fu

O-MEI MOUNTAIN Moon

Tonight a half-moon
rises over O-mei,

its pale light
floating on the river.

Leaving Ching-chi, the river plunges
through Yangtze gorge.

I sail on to Yu-chow,
thinking of you all the way.

—Li Po

NIGHT IN A ROOM by the River

Evening rises toward the mountain trails
as I climb up to my high chamber.

Thin clouds lodge along the cliffs.
A lonely moon rocks slowly on the waves.

A line of cranes flaps silently overhead,
and, far off, a howling pack of wolves.

Sleepless, memories of war betray me:
I am powerless against the world.

—Tu Fu

THE GREAT BIRD

When the Great Bird soars
his wingbeats rattle the world,
but even he cannot save himself—
he is broken in the sky.

Something of his essence
will linger through the ages.
He will catch his sleeve on the tree
at the edge of the world:

if you who come after
understand, pass it on.
With Confucius gone,
who will be left to mourn?

—Li Po

P'ENG-YA ROAD

I remember fleeing the rebels
through dangerous northern canyons,

the midnight moon shining bright
on narrow P'eng-ya Road.

So poor we went on foot,
we were embarrassed meeting strangers.

A few birds sang in the valleys,
but we met no one ever returning.

My daughter was so starved she bit me,
she screamed her painful hunger.

I clamped her mouth shut tight,
fearful of wolves and tigers.

She struggled hard against me,
she cried and cried.

My son was sympathetic
and searched the wilds for food.

Then five days of heavy rain arrived,
and we trudged through freezing mud.

We had no coats, no shelter,
we were dressed in cold, wet clothes.

Struggling, struggling, we made
but a mile or two each day.

We ate wild fruits and berries,
and branches made our roof.

Mornings we slogged through water,
evenings we searched for smoke on the skyline.

We stopped at a marsh
to prepare our climb to the pass,

and met a Mr. Suen,
whose standards are high as clouds.

We came through the dark
and lamps were lit, gates opening before us.

Servants brought warm water
so we could bathe our aching feet.

They hung paper banners
in our honor.

Mrs. Suen came out with all her children;
they wept for our condition.

My children slept, exhausted,
until we roused them with food.

Our host took a vow
he'd always remain my brother.

His home was made our home,
to provide for every comfort.

Who could imagine in such troubled times
he'd bare his heart and soul?

A year has passed since that fated night.
The barbarians still wage war.

If I had the wings of the wild goose,
I'd fly to be at his side.

—Tu Fu

*Ni Tsan (1301–1374): Trees in a River Valley at Yü-shan.
Hanging scroll, ink on paper (37 1/2 x 14 1/8"). C.C. Wang
Collection, New York.*

TO TU FU from Shantung

You ask how I spend my time:
I nestle against a tree trunk,

listening to autumn winds
in the pines all day and night.

Shantung wine can't get me drunk.
The local poets bore me.

My thoughts head south with you,
like the Wen River, endlessly flowing.

—Li Po

HEADING SOUTH

Spring returns to Peach Blossom River
and my sail is a cloud through maple forests.

Exiled, I lived for years in secret, moving on
farther from home with tear-stains on my sleeves.

Now old and sick, at last I'm headed south.
Remembering old friends, I look back north one final
    time.

A hundred years I sang my bitter song,
but not a soul remembers those old rhymes.

—Tu Fu

INDEX
TO THE
POEMS

Poems by Li Po and Tu Fu

Inklings Editions are a production of Weatherhill, Inc., publishers of fine books on Asia and the Pacific. Supervising editor: Meg Taylor. Book design and typography: Liz Trovato. Production supervision: Bill Rose. Text composition: G & H Soho, Inc., Hoboken, New Jersey. Printing and binding: Daamen, Inc., West Rutland, Vermont. The typeface used is Berkeley Old Style.